The White Beach

The White Beach

New & Selected Poems 1960 - 1998

Leland Bardwell

Salmonpoetry

Published in 1998 by
Salmon Publishing Ltd,
Cliffs of Moher, Co. Clare

© Leland Bardwell 1998
The moral right of the author has been asserted.

A catalogue record for this book is available from the British Library.

The Arts Council
An Chomhairle Ealaíon

Salmon Publishing gratefully acknowledges the
financial assistance of The Arts Council.

ISBN 1 897648 07 3 Softcover

Cover design by Brenda Dermody of Estresso
Cover illustration by Austin Carey
Set by Siobhán Hutson
Printed by Betaprint, Clonshaugh, Dublin 17

*For my family
and my extended family*

Acknowledgments

Some of the poems in this volume are taken from Leland Bardwell's first three collections: *Dostoevsky's Grave* (Dedalus Press, 1991), *The Fly & The Bed Bug* (Beaver Row Press, 1984), and *The Mad Cyclist* (New Writers' Press, 1970).

Acknowledgement is also due to the editors of the following publications, in which some of these poems first appeared: *Arena, Holydoor, Broadsheet, Poetry Ireland Review, Cyphers, and Force 10.*

Thanks to Fiona Carlin.

Other Books by Leland Bardwell

Poetry: *Dostoevsky's Grave* (Dedalus Press, 1991)
           The Fly & The Bed Bug (Beaver Row Press, 1984)
           The Mad Cyclist (New Writers' Press, 1970)

Novels: *There We Have Been* (Attic Press, 1989)
           The House (Brandon Books, 1984)
           That London Winter (Irish Co-op Books, 1981)
           Girl on a Bicycle (Irish Co-op Books, 1978)

Stories: *Different Kinds of Love* (Attic Press, 1987)
           (German trans.: Ullstein Taschenbuch, Berlin, 1991)

Plays: *Edith Piaf* (The Olympia, 1984)
           Open Ended Prescription (The Peacock, 1979)
           Thursday (Trinity College, Dublin, 1972)

Contents

Eighties

Nineties

Sixties

Kaleidoscope of Childhood in Ireland During the Emergency

I.
And the dead calf's head
was pinned to the foot
of the crib while the pony's ears
peeked over the stable door –
did blood drip down on the white-
washed rough-cast wall
while the pony's frightened eyes
explored the depths of the straw.
Oh, not a girl, the mother angry, cried
as the pelvis stretched again
to expel the afterbirth
Oh not a girl, a boy
might have merited suffering –
pain in the blackened ears like
song in the brain and she slid
her hands through the rumpled
crease of the stomach
flattened now after nine month's hard
like a marrow skin – and then
she knew that she'd get revenge
and call it boy and have it boy
and it would grow male and quick
not female soft that would spare
no-one but itself, and she sought
in her mind for a name that would suit
a boy – hard and generous –
a name of bird or gun
but a changeling, not to expect
affection – you're on your own
the mother, cynical, said

and the baby, cynical, moaned
the final female whinge and
papa banged down the phone.

II.
And the mother sedulously kept
the baby away from the breast
and bought a goat that gave
four pints of fine strong milk
a day – the fatted calf had been
a lousy joke of course it
was not born in a stable – oh
no – a damp and blood-stained bed
in some vast hygienic maternity
hall – delivered by rubber gloves
on a mid-wife's cruel mitts –
you do not scream to disturb
the delights of bearing a child
that you'll grow to hate –
and starve for the sex of pain
like a six inch nail in the head
so the brachyce phalic mite
screamed loud and raw and was
out of the shot of ears in a wooden
drawer removed to the top of the house
soon jumped or fell or crawled
from the home-made crib – and they
called it L as it leaned over carved
mahogany stairs that curved to the well
of the house and learned
to embrace the whims of an
adult world – in other words

to lie and kick with an ugly yell
that raised the roof
and then it hid till the guilt
expanded – it had to admit
that it was a boy – not natural –
and would not speak but learned
to read in the Latin tongue.

III.
And grandma – the dreadful threat
of shame – leaned over the cot
with the dangerous bars – no good
will come of this – she said
adjusting the iron grey squares
on her head – no pleasant place
ever housed a recalcitrant child
and she whipped her fist across
screaming maw and all the L's
rose up in side O it jumped from
the cot and snatched the text
Amor Dapis – I'll do it – I'll
have fun if it kills me – it said
and ran and now like fox-cubs
that caper it caught the wind
– the will o' the wisp – that
frightened the wits of the
other kids it sometimes saw
like a dream in the bed – alone I'll
break the valuable delph and
smash the truth from my mother's
ribs and it went to the topmost
branch of the scabrous apple tree

and spat on the distant adult complaints
futura – oh – don't climb up the
tree – it's true you might break
the branch.

IV.
At nine it walked in gentleman's clothes
and bore a gentleman's name, Lalande –
eighteenth century astronomer born
at Bourg 'un professeur eminent' –
he busied himself with the comets and
Mercury – Mercury – oh dear god of thieves
he prayed and robbed and lied
O Mercury, messenger of the gods
pay me I shall run I am
Lalande – to watch the stars and
born at Bourg – and I will pluck
the daisies from the grass
while the black dog licks
my cheek – now I am firm and fleet
my feet are narrow my limbs are
slender and strong – I will go
through galaxies and splash through
stars as the beach foam slaps the sand
and the stars will strike the earth
like tomorrow's space locked
and stored as time clocks in.

V.
Then indolence – indifference too –
and boredom clouds his mind – he seeks
relief in the cheap thin smoke
pennies snatched from his father's
coat – to hide and lurk in
the winter's grass – brown and curled
as an ancient book, slouched
in a ditch with a passing tramp –
How old are you son?
he answered eleven and offered a pull
on the damp bent fag – he smelled –
the tramp – like a dried sea bed
the boy called him Proteus and combed
the molluscs out of his tangled beard
He snuggled closer into the
sharp scutch-ditch
with the elderly seven-coated man
I love you Proteus – the boy now cried
and his feet could no more run
he'd got so heavy and drab
with the nicotine and the wet
grass drenched his limbs
I'm sunk, he said

VI.
and tiny breasts grew from
his narrow chest that long winter
and bombs fell on another island
The Emergency fell like a brick
all round. Lalande died, the star Mercury
messenger – thief fled into

7

the skies and the boy hid his breasts
and between his legs he put rags
which turned orange – red – then
black – and stank – and he threw
them over the hen-coup wire
dug half a hole in the muck,
in the yellow-smelling hen-shit –
It's happened, the mother said – No!
No! I deny, he answered – I cut my leg
on the netting wire and bowing like
an apostrophe he turned and ran again.

VII.
And now boy/girl it did not trust
it learnt new words like scavenge – poison
it put berries in its matted hair
it tied up the riverreeds and lay
under the snow-berries to burst
between finger and thumb and spurt
cream – it is cow-poison, see
it squelches like the udder
of the mad white cow that crosses
the moon – and money became as important
as the Latin homework and the lame
old dog – mongrel – that was Christened
Bran.

VIII.
Then at thirteen her name is
Lalage – she puts on long skinny
dresses with stripes – she wears

silk stockings and paints her
face in the bus from school –
she tenders half fare and smokes
behind filthy exercise books of don'ts
Do not cross the road
when you see the clergyman coming
Do not subsume your guilt
your hormones will split on you
Do not announce your equations
to the vigil-keeper – stone breakers
guides – ribbon men – you meet by
the way side. Do not do not – do not
open the book at the bus-stop it has
you by rote – it reads – there are
more than eight furlongs in the
eye long waste of seeing – two
perches
in the dried up shiboldth
of the adult mind – twenty-
hundred days in the tonal
monotony of adolescence Avoir du
Pois – weight – wait there is more
heavy stuff – nits in the hair that smells
of paraffin – black smears like hammer –
blows in the convex shelter
of the neck – legions of blackheads
down the delicate abrasion of the nose –
Oh noise – O – of thinking she's a girl
what must the boys – oh no – think of
her – luckily she knows none – a socio-
logical stratum about which a mist
of ignorance steams – you can keep them –

a speculation – like what the parents –
now almost human – I mean – with all
that chatter about politics – mean
I mean – do – do they ever – Oh no
the very thought of it!

IX.
Meanwhile the microscopic
nerve-cells – called neurons – of
which there are billions
systematically linked together – Nature
takes care – she murmured – chewing on
a Mars Bar – the wrapper caught –
hovered twirled fled on the wind – the
bus swerved – You may only enter
Paradise if – only enter Paradise if
you've been there before – when
she eloped from the bus she cried
Come all ye Yanks – war-dodgers – snivelling
mittle – European refugees – English
prisoners of war – Germans – On parole
from the sheep-short grass
of the Curragh – try me
I'm Locusta – known for my poisons
help-meet of Nero – and Laudice
        sometimes called
Electra – will with my brother –
two bit moralist – not under
any circs – try me I can ride –
swim – run – am fleet as a boy –was
a boy – I can play the piano and dodge
the fine rain that falls lightly

on my Latin mistress – Amo –
Miss White – Amo – Miss White Pulchra
est – Irish boys are hell –
but only the wind flapped answer and
the hemiptera made sucking sound
on the tight white skin of her skull.

X.
Now she curled in the circum-
volution of the dog-eared books –
there was catharsis if you like
– not the night bell clang of the church
clock reminding you'll not make the
early bus – fat tallow on the pillow –
case under Poe – Tales of Imagination –
or – worse still – the game is
– the game is – up – not worth
the candle – Kafka F., Dostoevsky F.
have snuffed it Rosa Luxembourg and those
hard working Italians who fought for
the poor were stuffed or topped or
burnt by electricity – Millions
of volts according to State – Ho America
our new big movie-scene Mitch for Garbo
Claudette America of the automobile
apartments – ice-boxes – elevators
foxy little husbands eaten by
big fat Blue Haired Mommas
T. Williams – E. O'Neill
TELL ALL – come to Leixlip
we'll sell you anything from
a bull dozer to a bull terrier dear –

O dear – dear America you are over –
doing it – you've more cars
eat more bright red beef
than anywhere else put together
and two billion dollars spent on cos-
metics – lips – cheeks – eyelashes
as unlikely as a mid-wife's sex-
fantasies – powder paint lip-
stick – brushed on delicately not
jammed on like we do it – two Donald
Ducks kissing on the cartoons
perms – straighteners – grease – eye-
shadow – and all those lovely shan-
gri la creams/Tir na n'Og here
I came watch those lines wrinkles
psoriasis spots – tumours cancers
lifted like magic plain envelope results guaranteed we'll
comb out your
body odour – note the spelling –
we will exterminate breasts –
babies – or any other
minor growth or irritation
Phew Satan – consider me an applicant
for a new lease of life.

XI.
And so Satan – so cunning said
You've asked for it I'm punning
on the highway with the great Cave
boy – Clergyman's son – myopic
barely – but clean with pointed ears
like bat's wings – there's things

12

you should know about, baby – he's
not Gary Cooper or even James Mason
much less Raskolnikov – but he'll give it
to you hot and proper in his Trinity
rooms – zooms – Lalage – Laodice – dark-
robed Leto – Lucretia – the lot arrived
panting – not to be kept waiting another
second in stained-brown gym-tunic late
for school ready to overlook all poss-
ible flaws in the execution of her De-
flowering – capital letter – better
never than late – what a let-down
and no bed just the tea stained
draining board or else the floor – cold –
you've said it – I've changed my mind
my grandfather is dead – Today
is the Ides of April the month of Venus – Quam
pulchrissimam Virgonem he said crunching her narrow
bones and scattering them
on the hard floor Tomorrow – she
cried – I'd die sooner – Domani
e troppo tarde – he said – You've
a nerve – she said simulating courage
of a last minute variety – Piety
was never your strong point – he
said – reverting to English – I'm off
she said. She went – Back to Satan
said – There's some mistake – I
don't seem to go for it after all
I guessed you'd be like that Satan
replied his face creaming over
with a wily smile – how much your soul's
quarter then for old Beelzebub – eh?

Annihilated yet curious she murmured I
Locusta ought to have a career
Love-squeaked Satan – ten decibels
later she said – What about
shorthand-typing? Love squeaked
the fork-tailed menace – no no – anything
else – a trip to Venice after
the war – meanwhile my Inter-inter
alia – Ha ha – you'll never pass
your Irish is terrible.

XII.
But unfortunately that thick
word truth will out she'd
as usual lied did not – in fact –
say what she thought she had – let alone
pretended to herself – the devil and
all his works – that she's said
she had not said any of the above
things to the original cave-boy Trinity
raper in chief for fair play Tarquinius
Lucretia vim – ha – attulit
on the highway she in fact had lacked
the courage to refuse and now nightly
prayed – Lord – don't let it happen
There are always the Cliffs of Moher
no-one ever jumped backwards
up those grey-flensed Ireland's
answer to the New York State Building
another eighteen days before I'll
know for certain – and Jesus –
what about Grandma?

XIII.
The sunshine strikes ricochets on
the gay gun-metal pavement in College
Green – eyes right – like a Scout –
girl – Lalage – regazza – better
Laodice – but fears Orestes now older
student – falconer – lurking over
the sister's guilt – O Agamemnon O
Clytemnestra she shouts to the
dead blue sky while scurrilous clouds
play hill and cheek with the sunstriped
warning – all normal people scurrying
late – but pure – no crippling dread –
she – to everyone of them a load –
an eyesore – embarrassment – Grafton Street
Mitchells thin feet scudding hard –
O Woolworth's land of ear-rings and
brooches – bangles heavy with charms –
one for every birth day – one –
for her a fish – pelucid sea –
Nereis – daughter of Neptune receive me
your wet arms will stroke me like strings
of emerald beads – wind them about
my body till the dead weed drags me
down in the depth of your rock
swollen like water forced from
the earth by the satellite Icarus
until a false god will cry Noah
save the clean ones – but Laodice
cries to be her own her brother to
become again a boy and when the moon
is round and she is free – she

will once more squander her limbs to
the crazy air – tinker – daughter of sand
son to the sunflower – tropist and
she will turn to the burning orb –
barb – needle or hazel-stick twin to
herself entwined in the freedom of
trading form with mind – tendering
each delicate hair – thin foliole ray –
to breathe – to go faster than sound
than light – than gravity –
then no lecherous grave will shout
her names – Locusta will live
Laodice – Leto – of the night
Even Lucretia – but mostly will
the astronomer Lalande – of Bourg
arise to bless his birth O
how pale and full and sure
is the moon that slides in
the purple night – night star
of morning Venus – his aide –
guide of mariners – hour long vigil
of fear to devouring hope – life IS
when death breaks foul in the mouth
like an old man's failing gasp. Turn
like time from the tortured lips
of the wrinkled hag.

XIV.
But sun she is sunflower – tropist –
and turns again – back to the wind –
dark sea – subsumation of still wind
weed and fissure – a gin – adread

of scorn – pleasure of need – O
she will want and want – desire is the
drought that blames the desert – reflecting
men who build of sand and thunder
the burial bans to the gaunt and silent mob.

XV.
And then there was freedom of a kind
dark circle of dread evicted from
the mind – the moon had fled
Laodice sought herself – her real
brother Orestes – they will revenge
the father's death in a child-worn
mind – soon or never – but
will one day join – now she waits
on the drydock's edge
the sledge hammer beats like a gong
in her head – one day they will
sing me Electra – but now I
am boy again – brother sister – all –
I am – Orestes – he sings as he tried
the bridle paths and lies in the
shade of elm and beech – never
again will they catch him out
he bows to magpie and calls to
thrush – bluebird carrion or winter crow
learns to whistle and tread like
a boy – hands in pockets – lurch and
kick – What an atrocious piece of luck he
says – subsides in a ditch with a book.

Message for Dickie

'*Goodbye little yellow bird*'
– Victorian Musichall song

Here is a sort of conspiracy
a poem that will steal around you
like your lover's arms.
A poem, without literary sentences,
that might only hover and pick at the truth
like moths around Marlene Dietrich.

I love you, Richard
like I love old steam trains
and the memory of beer bottle tops
sticking to the carpet
in Lower Leeson Street.
You know that freedom
is something for the birds
and if once in a while
you open the cage of the canary
they'll throw the square root
of bureaucracy at you
and they'll strap you
on to the metal horses
and absent minded stereo sounds
will make the fifth ending.

The Mad Cyclist

The wind blew West from the sun
on the force of the oncoming peddler
at 400 revs per m.
Exceeding the navicular limit
she steered through the middle
of buses and hot summer skins
of the addle of stammering sex
and the men with wallets
that split at the seams
and are worn like life preservers.

This fantoccini on wheels
was clean as their short plump limbs
harboured sweat in the toes of their socks;
she was fast as the slow dawning leers
disguising their political cramps;
and funny, flashing past like the Enterprise
bringing the business men in
in merciless Mondaying manner
as they, behind blocked in a row
who, thanks to their waterless tanks,
were shrunken and human piranha.

Such arrogance must be prevented
such unnatural practices stopped
or have her certificated
for putative felo-de-se
but she with her revs circumvented
their aims and cried 'ou est mon velo'
like Cocteau to Diaghialev
when the latter said 'J'suis Ètonné.

    And she sped past
    left them astonished
    with the swoon of her pupils

balancing her country pride
on a mirage de convenance.

Then we'll have her obfuscated
in the quicksands of modern suburbia
they conceived a magnificent plot
of creating a labyrinth
in an anonymous building estate
and providing a motorised minotaur
which sooner or later should eat her.

But she threaded her way
through the eye
with miraculous wisdom
descending the hill
the latest escarpment
of souls in cement
(her movements inclining to skill).

Yet in spite of her feral intensity
she chose to despair
on a wintry night in July
the moment that Aldrin and Armstrong
stepped off the moon.
She steered her base-metal bicycle
out of the sterile orb
and bumped in the rut she was in
to the last still lake that made light
leaving the tarry academized snake

propounding a theory
that everything might have been bought with a bike
if time had allowed her to think.
With the final escalibrous flash
of the handlebars
the jewels of poverty sank.

Cinema '68

In the movies the goodies got the witch
they belted her with moral superiority
so she got the hell out;
the sound men and the sparks had had a ball
and the director stopped tearing up paper
while he thanked everyone.
They folded their gear and took it
beyond the essence of believing.

In the dust and dark of the studio
the ghosts of the copulating couples
settled down to acknowledge
the past as valid; although
freedom was a better lie.

    The director went out into winter
    so tired he could barely move
    the trees leaned on him like sick vultures
    he was fed-up making B movies.

    The following day he rose at 5;
    he tore up six unit call-sheets
    and the menu for yesterday's lunch;
    he got on the blower to his backer
    and upped his expenses £2000.

    He was on the set at the dot of six
    (the unit and the cast had fierce hangovers)
    especially the female lead.

    The director was relentless:

Learn your lines on the marriage bed, mistress,
lie well and hide your mercy under the mattress.
(Page one of the script; the basic four-letter
suffering invented by tubercular Egyptian princes
5000 years B.C.)

So, because you understand
you have invented a game:
blind-man's-bluff in the hall of mirrors
if the bandage slips they'll see your eyes,
frightened, accusing or acquiescent,
but never understanding
they don't know you understand
there's no reflection in the mirror.

If love has been killed by love
it is hidden like crystal into water
take it smooth from the river
and warm the crystal in your palm;
name it.
You will give out puffs of perfume
like the daughters of the rich
then summer will kill the flowers
and the black grass pencils, the horizon.
You will put your blood on the rod
and say 'carry away the birth,
the birth is yours'
and dry your hands in the fire
if the blood has stained the sheets.

Proteus changed his costume
for the nth time, saying
'some people are never satisfied.'
The female lead screamed 'it's a lie,
a stupid lie. Who do you think you are?
Fellini? Bergman?'
The day wore on as planned;
the crowd extras yawned
into overtime.

The director embraced his chihuahua;
now that he was going to be famous
he had nothing to live for;
he had torn up the flooring
of his Mercedes 230 S.E.
and the extended budget by mistake.

He went into the empty studio
and squelched round on the flat sausage rolls
he overheard a conversation being conducted
by one of the copulating couples,
heretofore mentioned;

'Now that the movie is re-wound
what'll you do
Prisoner of the Snow Queen?
Will you melt at your brother's kiss?

'No, that'd be too warm.'
'Will you wash the dead horse

and stretch the skins in the sun,
rider?'
'No, that'd be too healthy.'

'Will you cut the shroud on the cross
so that it hangs well,
seamstress?'

'No, it might look like a loin cloth.'

    The director cast round for some paper
    but the sparks had thrown the main switch
    (it wasn't his job to know what that was)
    he made a mental note to change his psychiatrist;
    this therapy was tedious.
    He asked the copulating couples to shut up a minute
    so as he could get his bearings;
    then he threaded his way through the broken
        paper cups
    and the leads from the dead brutes;
    he ripped up his clothing;
    feeling no better, he died.

There was a tremendous funeral;
the company was drunk for a week.
The female lead went to bed with the wardrobe master
by mistake; she thought he was Proteus;
the newsmen never had it so good.

Months later some joker wrote on his tombstone
        'Understanding blew his mind.'

Flowers for the Three Dead Men

I.   was a low-sized lad from Belfast
Who made me along the quays
On a night and a day against
Arm or winch or spar
Or something cold like a midnight steel
Where a seagull dips
And waters discreetly lap
As the Liffey's lazy mouth
Yawns into a sea.
We kipped in a B. & B.
The following night
Between sheets where emigrants
Flea-blood spots were
Each like a tache or mote;
There we mingled for twelve hours full
Till a lady in lavender dress
Announced time was up.
A dread to a girl; besides
He was drunk when he left.

II.   the best, was a Norfolk man – a host
To his loves, all surl and sex
Like a black-skinned man on a furl.
A giant 6ft. 3 in his socks.
He spoke not of love for speaking destroys
(He was intelligent as well!)
Yet we sailed by a moon on a cirrus dream
With Icarus wings for seven years
Till the sun.

III. had it away with my friends,
Delightful in a daisy-way
But this limited our relationship
And debt did us part.

Tiny lifeless anemone hurts.

To Robert MacBryde, Died May 1966

As each one is guided by his own mad star
So, Robert, too soon hurled into the night.
Your feet, leaf-light, side-stepped too late.

Chaining history to your Achilles Shield,
Fashioned by your one-god, Hephaistos,
Who yet extracted for his grasses your wild flowers.
Like gazing from a Míro to a mirror.

Thus did you have to wander always
And alone were by wonder driven.

Dance Robert, nowhere now,

All is forgiven.

Returning Home

She returned to the house, the house, the house
where she was born, grew into her brothers' clothes
and fought the enemies.
Where the iron bed
was a Sultan's gate
where Gaugin's Polynesian wife
hung from the scabrous apple tree
and the last bus missed and the hinges shrieked
and the flags were cracked and the stairway creaked.

She'd return to the house
with the answering ass and the putrid tank
the slimey strawberry-coloured sides
where she'd slithered in in her brother's clothes
and was afraid to go in with the dreadful stink
that rose from her garments
covered in autumn leaves

She'd see the old place again
to get the necessary pang
that would subsidise her normal pain.
Fine, she thought, fine,
the place will have fallen, anyway.

She approached the town planning.
The new road pressed in, a tidal wave,
factories fanning aggressively;
boxes of precision, a hemisphere
of no-man's land.
Teenagers rushed out with love in their buckets
to pour on her shadow and the houses
bowed to her sightless and closed.

At last the house,
the granite stones had been scrubbed
pointed – 0 Moon, 0 Jaguar
22 litres, 80 degrees from the door
0 apple green Georgian asphalt drive
crush her feet! She pressed the bell.
Who shall I say – a voice from hell.
Who indeed, she said. We don't drown, it said
only burn, but step inside.

Her host sat naked under a sun ray lamp.
Yes? he said with a masterful smile.
Its just my lies, she said, I left behind
I can't have them lying around all over the place
He laughed at her pun, Pernod?
he suggested hostfully
his body dappled with healthy tan,
I'm a man, he said, thumping his breast.
I'll make you an offer for the best lie,
she said. Your happy past?
he asked. By now he was dressed
a business man to his socks –
his lips the cream of a wily smile.
How much? A barrel of winter charm
a dead rat and a rusty nail.
Done, he said, and took her arm.

Locked in his Jaguar power dream
She would go his way
to the speculator's dead man's hole
where he prized his life
to its iron grey soul.
She laid her head on his £100 shoulder.
Never. He drew to a stop.
The plan of the engine is God.

For the Shade of F. Scott Fitzgerald

Etiolated, I climb up each morning
from my basement in Low Leeson Street,
sometimes it is afternoon when I surface.

Where things are normal for a few
at street level, the sun perhaps may shine
but warmth can be bought
by cheque book or tongue.

I stand aside in shops
making my fiscal offerings
for necessities,
remembering the givers and the takers
are always with us
with their patterns and their graphs.

It is safer to laugh at the patient
whose lovers may get angry
if their breakfast is also late.

Leixlip and The Rye

Leixlip, my first and great and only love,
I wish I could describe the street
just house by house.
Or first the largest squarest Georgian
which they messed with pipes outside;
a wasted garden back and front.

Or begin with the bridge
before the hydro-electric scheme
shut off the water, dirtied its bed
and left a tray of weeds.

From the bridge, the castle
gay in places, different faces
of granite dragged by local labour;
a tiny harbour for the castle boat.

But no-one wrote about the Rye;

The Liffey, in every loving curve
is praised so much (leave out
the Salmon Leap, which now
is quite a pleasant engineering feat
while salmon must go underneath
to spawn.)

Wondering wandering tributary
whose source lies somewhere near Kilcock.
Through your valleys and Moyvalley
watering Carton's gardens,
all the Dukes of Leinster washed;
an Empress jumped you once.

You crushed out the gravel
under the royal canal
driving a bargain into the fields of Confey.
And there at the castle gates of Leixlip
roared your allegiance with the Liffey
with the little bridge at the castle gates,
a pub on either side,
where a lady ran guns in the troubles
and other ladies cried,
watching their Georgian mansions crumble;
a humble stream that cut their Anglo-Irish meadows
with reeds and dragon flies and otters,
who played briefly in their reason.
And the ladies waited patiently
for the start of the hunting season.

For Ruth Ellis

In Camden Street, London, N.7
And that was long before
Marching became the norm
A brisk watery sun
Rose, surly, on a bank of trees.

As hysteria mounted,
Took over the precinct
Like a burning house
In the mess of dogs
And bulging rubber faces.
The schoolkids mitched
Bursting into the clamour
With their clear morning faces
Like soap-bubbles in the sun.
Crying 'REPRIEVE'
And half of them did not know
The meaning of the word. –

In the breakfast of their equal loss

The Queen
The Home Secretary
And Ruth Ellis
Had eaten well.

That was the latest news
SENSATIONAL.

Please Mr. Pierrepoint
Another lover died outside a Hampstead pub

Who took the trade of dalliance and sport;
But eternity plays in a jealous mart;
We kill for stupidity, not for love.

But behind the useless bulging of that oaken door
Somewhere, undefeated, the hangman stands,
Immutable as a snowman.

If her rope is a makeshift cross
What good comes out of a tragedy that's pure
Or a comedy that's harsh?

Seventies

Children's Games

Once upon a time
I saw my two children playing
where Karl Marx was lying
with a tombstone on his head;
they were naked from the waist down

and the English around and around said
'Better the children dead
than naked from the waist down.'

Now I was a foreigner
on that cold Highgate Hill
but I bore no ill to the English
no ill.

So I toiled away by the Spaniards
where the English were all lovers
and their legs gleamed O
so cold and naked
naked from the waist down

and I tried another graveyard
and found another plot
where Sigmund Freud was lying
in his eiderdown of weeds

'My children,' I said, 'romp away
this little strip is yours
for the dead are mostly idle
and do not care if you are naked
naked from the waist down'.

and the graves began to smile
and the hymn of England fade
and my children took out their pocket knives
and carved on the limey stone:

Dr Freud lies here in the nettles
we are dancing on his head.

Has Elizabeth Shaved Her Head?

Has Elizabeth shaved off
her hair; Has Elizabeth
sent it to her

sailor boy? Rock-a-bye
sailor round the rolling
deep; roll my able

bodied man. Is her head
as bald as a question
mark? Is her head

at all lovely now
sailor? Do you want
to bend the sea

with your weight? Dive for the
herring bone weave
on the dark henna

plait? O sailor boy
rock on the rolling
deep for mad Elizabeth

is dead. Do you shock
easily sailor,
do you shock? For

mad Elizabeth took
the bowls from her
eyes with an iris-stroke

and folded her long
barren body; she folded
up tight like a butterfly

after its life's day's
done. Sailor fill
your vessel, fill it like

a whale and skim skim
the waves like a waltz
Elizabeth does not wait

living; does not cast
her net now, sailor
the coast is clear.

The Limerick graveyard
ticks its tock; morning
opens its silver

mouth; will you dock
easy, sailor,
will you dock?

Prison Poem II

Dawn lifts its blue-veined face
    slaps the chimney, slides down,
    disappears beyond the kitchen.

Seagulls, fulmars, kittiwakes
    freewheel for a frenzied dive.

Dawn has spoken, has cried
    Kyow, kyow, kyawk.

Day shakes out its dirty shirt;
    sleeves whisper, 'They've sold us down the river.'

Afternoon half rises, inert, polite.
    It soon is left for dead.

Night straps down its quilt
    Forces the colours behind our eyes.

We believe!
    Like children believe
    in the tall words of their picture books.

Prison Poem V

This way madam! Miss, Mrs, Ms. It's all the same
In the darkened corridor, in the elbow of orange light
Shed by the penitentiary bulb.

She even feels a seam of pity
For the unhappy puzzle on the young cop's face
But she knows she could pedal the flowers of friendship
Till the cows went home and she'd only learn one fact:
He hates her.

For this is the way of things;
Not only is she in the wrong, she is a woman.
The tremble of God's eyelid wouldn't open
Or storm the Bastille of his mind.
How has he sunk so low as to have to walk
With such an evil thing?

Her own identity is something left behind
With generous other days on dirty Dublin streets
Like watching the sad expression on her landlord's face
Or fixing the metre quickly before it's read
Or even a morning queuing for the dole.

But the crash of the heavy lock resounds;
The childhood mortice of an unknown room
And she is again a child on whom fleshless silence
Clamps its morbid teeth.

She lies under the weight of it
In the air that's as cold as salt and with her stare
Breaks up the surface of the cobbled wall
Beneath whose cloak of dust, graffiti, blood,
A million creatures whisper; with or without her
Their parliament is never still.

And Hyde House Comes Tumbling Down

Business is business
(Death and destruction).

I watched from my yard
(Hyde's one time stables)
the building sway, resettle,
the bulldozers haul
on the oil-grimed cable
A mooring and warping
It was almost gentle –
an old craft
in the smallest push of wind –
the dust settle, too
like a pile of coats.

Speculators drum up
vibrations of a past life
(an excuse for a heart-shaped plaque)
and with their destroyer's toys
thump and wallow –
the glutinous mud is infertile –
hippos without
melancholy innuendo.

Nearon

Nearon saw only his sister
At the corner of Hatch
and lower Leeson street.
She looked a treat that day
in her shock-white blouse and mini skirt
(You'd never know from here
she was over forty.)

Nearon saw only his sister,
nine years old, he six
she held his hand, said 'Hurry,
Nearon or we'll miss the band
in Stephen's Green.' The camber
slapped the soles of his feet
and the band played Waltzing Matilda.

You Always Have Your Children

You always have your children
they say as though you'd tried
to look a gift-horse in the mouth.
As if you carried this layer
of protection on your back
(an extra layer) unlike the common man.

But your sons blaze brightly
in the bonfire of their youth
while naked as a fish between two banks
you cower between the generations

On your death bed you imagine
you'll raise your head like a gun
your nerve ends quivering
like the needles of a compass
and say you once saw Paul Durcan
at the end of the Western World
making sandcastles for his daughters
and you shouted:

Over to you boy, the inquisition,
the saturnine raven of love.

Michelangelo's David and Me

In the middle was the Renaissance
  God the rapacity
In the middle was myself
  Anonymous

I confound
  This labour of vanity
    Method, intention, protestation
    The divine molecules
      The continuity of marble

My identity quickens
  Forty-five in Florence
  Fathoms of heat
  I am alone

I have been infinitely caused
  Compass and clock
  I am polymorphous
  organised, cornered

This is the city of stone
  Called serene
Slow greys
  of the Medici Palace
By this stone
  Dignity prospers

I strayed in this city
    where time has no layers
    I have slain Goliath
    Am responsible
       For Santa Croce

The David's gaze
    is anglepoised above my head
    The cotton cloth
    of a faltering nun
    has stroked my calf,
    Her robe describes
    a rustling circle
    a movement of envy
    and hunger.

Working Wife's Return.

I.
His root is like a horse-radish
and raging in his petticoats
he stalks the garden-god
behind closed blinds.

Darkness everywhere
She gropes around.
She has nothing to give
except the shavings from her head.

She shakes it and the sawdust trembles
in her open brain; smells sweet
as hospitals. While the ever-present
mice hatch numerous plots.

It is dreary scraping the egg yolk
from the table cloth; more vainly dreary
when the jam is mixed with Bartok
and Berlioz and the piano
is clogged with semen.

Dear God, could he not sweep up
in her absence? Then she might consider
a return to his rock-hard socks.

II.
If there were ever anything to shut out
at night
Sigh-like or love or even the stars
to stay bright
even though every crevice is thick with dust.
If there were a welcome to wear away the time.

But just the sledge-hammer of the television
in the interval before the stalk to bed
the armhold of sleep while he raises ructions
reading yesterday's Sunday Times
and then the lean over into the edge of night
the deep ravine of the mattress, sperm matted
fag-filled
the sky-grey sheets wrinkled and pillows
pilloried.

If there were even a few failed snores
to complain about
under the nostrils' quiver,
she'd be the first home like Red-riding hood
going to her grandmother.

Fantasies and Heroes

Visions like trains
Visions like trains

I shed blood
for a wounded consciousness
like a hungry hippie
on the Himalayas,
for injustice injustices,
Tensing tensing
on the Southern col.
The muscles calling
calling for love
like the raging Ganges.
Red is the river
dead is the taker.
I sell the silk
of Genghis Khan
and gallop away
on a wild white horse
on the Steppes of Mongolia.

Up the steps of the
White House, only
passing through thanks,
thanks to the tea
I've just taken
with S.J. Perrelman
and Father So and So, S. J.
on Madison Avenue
have a new one on me
Groucho; O no

I mean Marilyn
Marilyn Monroe.
Please let me share
your shy little pills for

Visions like trains
Visions like trains

We'll ride on the cow-catcher
of the Canadian Pacific
holding the smile of
Buster Keaton
holding the smile
till we get to Moscow

and challenge Kosygin
to a duel with Pushkin,
Lermontov is dying
in the forests of Cuba
and Franz Kafka is waiting
in the groin of the tuba
of Jelly Roll Morton.
And south further south
from the tears of N'Orleans,
under the shadow
of Popocatapetl
I'll never do with Lowry
what he never did.

My blood's in the arrows
of Montezuma
and its cold in the south
and love is howling.
The pemican's gone,
and the ponies dead.
Captain Oates is out walking
and may be some time
but our snow-blind eyes see

Visions like trains
Visions like trains.

Sally Anne

Sally Anne, Sally Anne
    thin as a tooth pick, Sally Anne
    teased she was and ran from a will o' the wisp
    and married a man with a book of cheques.

Sally Anne, Sally Anne
    looked back once (that was her downfall)
    she was so far away from her feet
    like Alice in Wonderland.

Then they buried Sally Anne
    in a coffin as black as a bowler hat
    but long before the lid was dust
    she'd wormed her way out.

Sally Anne, Sally Anne
    has no plan now – she wings on a jigsaw
    she lies flat on a mat on the floor
    of an unmade bargain.

Sally Anne, is a lazy broad
    she says she's trying to find the other piece
    of sky that was lost like a trick
    but that's a lie.

What will they do with Sally Anne?
    Some people think she's thick
    others say she's a thief and a cheat
    but she's on nobody's conscience which is a relief.

The Adventures of Orpheus and Euridice

I.
And Orpheus said
I can't play cache-cache
under the table
for the rest of my life
while Euridice's puns
couldn't keep up with
Orpheus travelling in front of time.
So she dressed up in a fraction
and waved her tight arse
which she had neatly halved
for the occasion.

The shrinks gathered round
and shook their learned forelocks.
They were dressed in whole numbers
like motor-cycle cops.
(Their faces had come into fashion.)
But they couldn't find her hiding
beneath the piano
while Orpheus composed a new song
called 'I am the last of the romantics
and the last romantic to admit it.'

II.
Orpheus' harp sang back at him
so he flipped the coins
and every coin he tossed
fell harps; angry, he hurled
the cash at the barman
who blandly rang the till
'Who am I to Gatsby, who
is he to me,' the barman said.

Meanwhile Euridice
had sent her brittle pawns
across the enemy lines.
They returned with the news
of a dog with three pink tongues.
'Is that all you have to tell me?'
she said. But the shrinks
who had all turned into chessmen
fell on their sides laughing.
So she ran backwards through the swollen bars
counting the faceless names
for she had so interpreted
their instructions. And the further
back she went, the further
away the sunset. When she arrived
at the hamburger queue, the notice
at the hatch said:
You mustn't get carried away

III.
Then Orpheus
entered the depths
as far down as a day's sleep.
He passed the glaziers
the quondam haymakers
on holiday from the Elysian fields
they carried horses
on their shoulders.

He had had the dream
neither cauchmar
white horse, nor reality.

He had followed the river
up the mountain.
Had elbowed out of line
the transient myth.
He had bathed his skin
in the water, and the water
was soft. Soft as folly
played at the end
of a heartstring.

Euridice was gone now,
gone from the song –
the poem – the steps
down the poem were long
the footfalls on the poem
were as silent as pollen
falling on mushrooms.

He had taken Euridice's queen,
for the last time
he had dressed in her queen,
her black queen,
her white queen,
he had broken the rules
with bad lines
and false moves.

So he withdrew into time,
and time danced in his favour,
time broke the barriers of doom
and the barriers of light
and numbers.

Whole numbers would come and go
and whole numbers squared
would again square other numbers,
dance numbers, like the island
that dances in the waves,
away beyond the headland
of motor-cycle cops
headshrinkers
beer bottle tops
cigarette butts
half-empty tins.

The army of mice
who play tip and swim
with the well water,
typewriters
that soak up sweat
lost from drinking whiskey.

'Leave your kisses,'
Euridice had said,
'Hermes is a nice guy
who plays a song called, chase
on a borrowed guitar.'
'Hermes is a secret
and splendid fellow,'

Orpheus had agreed – 'Who'll
keep my tears to augment
the waters of Lethe?'

IV.
So Euridice said, 'O.K. Death,
spare the yardstick
and spoil the memory.'
'I'll give you the waters of Lethe,'
Death said, shaking his
Euclidean locks.
'Terror dries the saliva in my mouth,'
she said, 'and I must drink.'
But the pebbles beneath the surface
shone clear like children's faces.

'But you are here to die,'
Death said, laughing.
'It's no laughing matter,' Euridice said.
Then Orpheus pressed his fingers
into his gloves.
When the splintering mirror
reflected Hermes again
as some kind of angel,
he laughed too.

'Give me the green mountain,'
Orpheus said.

Far Roamed Leto In Travail To See If Any Land Would Be A Dwelling For Her Child

for Jacky

Leto screwed in Paris
within her grey sea
inalienable element.
She lived on garlic
and donkey mince.

There in the screwing
a little calcium was absorbed.
The depth of a nail or
a hollow tooth; tinker
tailor soldier etcetera.
What'll it be a girl or
twins? The sins of ...

She screened her mind like Nijinsky.
In Geneva or Zurich they go
to go mad or die.

She went down the Boul'miche
in the sorrow of her skirt.

C'est ni Communiste ni Catholique
guns and bathos and bad jokes
copied from Prevert.
Later the slogan went
*C'est ni Communiste ni Catholique
ni Prevert.*

Leto died with Malone
came like a Miro poster
and played the games that Genet
played. In for a penny in for a pound.

But Leto mainly manless
took the painless foetus
to London down Highgate Hill
like Dick Whittington with his bundle.
They hadn't invented the pill
only the telephone and the jungle
and drums beat in her head
like hollow moons.

She resisted Regents Park
where the hexagonal arses
of business men had smoothed
the benches and allowed Americans
to suck the white motes from her fingernails
till she became as shapeless as a marrow.

Leto waited for the birth of Artemis,
white dancer in the womb.

Part II

Leto's travails are over.
Artemis' spacious dance
fills the horizon.
Pythian Apollo lays his golden blade
beside him.

Hera listens to this intelligence
with cynical ear.
Delos receives you with importunities
and blackmail.

You think you have paid amply for each child
by the circles on your belly;
to make your heart a brass foundry
of noises and shapes.

For every witch a devil; and the
devil you know is better than ...

Leto laughs at the thought
of Hera's potential anger.
Some small absurdity of time
is no measure of knowledge
and habit is the shadow of fake ...

But Hera has lost her sense of humour
not her power. She bides her time.

Come Sleep in Cancer Ward

Bleached squares of immaculate linen
subside like unmanned parachutes
hard-working hands inquire into the contours of
    your body
this is a quiet trauma and to be dealt with as such;
they must not find out about the internal rage
that rots inside you like the stump of an old tree
killed by frost.
They are so kind, these ministering angels; their hands
are so democratically efficient; herself heedless
of this kindness blames them for they are the nearest
to hand
and as with the doctors' intelligent eyes she strains
for their sympathy; saying with hers:
pity me not, for I am intelligent too
the goddess Athene cannot guide me as a woman
for I have journeyed too far on this nightmare voyage
my craft carries too much disloyalty
the men fight in the galleys; their blunt oars
only skirt the fractious waves; the boat describes
an arc and the tiller rasps on the rocks
there's no radar screen to gauge these dangerous rocks
that lurk like killer sharks with blue fins silently
savouring their limitless element;
someone must be blamed or the night won't bring that
heavy sleep,
sleep that drags life with claws,
that strains to hold the body
to dream or float in a solid water of silence,
silence that seeps,
that oscillates with its own particular forms
pentagrams like stars – not real stars,

pictures of stars in a planetarium.
The ceiling gets further and further away
recedes in these waves that are moving forms.
There is now a fleet of ships sidling along;
some sort of electric storm has blown up
and the sides of the flotilla are bruised and blasted.

The sea is everywhere now; the sea is the sky,
is beautiful. A rolling darkness upon darkness
time used to have some value, could be divided up
could be pared like a pencil into a fine intensive point
the sea used to be the sea and the sky the sky
then there was a plane a mountain a house
and the houses were divided too; there were lofts
and basements and places with square indentations
where doves went, where doves could sit and make
    contented
the warmth of their fluffy bodies, a little heat
like a little death beats against human hand
that makes fear; the instinct selects the absolute;
something for the alchemist who turns base metal
    into gold.

There must be some mistake, allow me to leave,
    she says,
I have been directed to the wrong place.
It sometimes happens that these mistakes, too,
are made on purpose.
But the doctors have chosen words for this kind
    of happening;
they have giant tomes and little books
and hippocratic ethics and all sorts of rules
which work perfectly for the golden mien;

Medusa can seek revenge for Perseus; she has broken
     the mirror,
the kaleidoscopic morsels make pretty remnants;
so natural as they twirl to catch the light
with small respect indeed for such pursuits
as make a cult of bravery
as if bravery were a stage in existence – like youth –
that everyone experiences,

Or she can say she is Nereus, daughter of Neptune
and call it a day.
Lightly lightly drift downward even pretending a little
that she really enjoys the taste of seaweed;
the scraping of bone on crustacea
the rocks full of stinking mortality,
but there are cliffs to be established,
cliffs that rear up like sheets of metal in the skin of
     a mist
they are luminaries; they have reason and established
     positions.

They are the almoners who count your money
and make little pencil ticks against varied loss;
they list the guests and slice the thin lemon
into the glasses. It is so perfectly selected,
no room for gatecrashers, for the bums
who steal your possessions and drink your wine.
You must not join in the singing,
make magic like marriage plans,
the honeymoon to be spent in olive groves
where sun and shade are equally divided.
Moreover they are so perfect they will admit mistakes

will disarm you with apologies, explain these things
    can happen
in this way with the manners of priests
they may momentarily convince you that they
    understand
and are not an army gone mad from killing.

But their subtlety fails for the occupying army
steals for the sake of stealing; takes the transistor
and fires it into the nearest ditch
for its weight is not worth the carrying.
You have learnt these brand new shining truths
as they dish them out,
you will pass the examination with credits in every colour
and then slip away, evaporate almost before their
    very eyes,
till your shadow becomes a stain on the wall.
They are sardonically surprised that it could possibly
    become unclear
unclear like memory that adjusts itself to imagination.

Master Proust himself could hardly better
this situation. You will sink into a glowing nadir
each moment of sensuality a bubble that is isolated
and lives for one fraction of a second before bursting.
There are all sorts of possibilities, like masturbation
or the reading of books about mental health;
the True Way through foods that are organically grown;
dozens of quacks to whet your appetite to re-assure
    you,
or simply walking to the Holy Land in your stocking feet
or Lourdes or any old place stuffed with tourists,
on quick-way cheap returns as angry and dirty as yourself;

just the same as business men in the London
    underground
who do the same thing every day
with the same discomfort,
because they really believe they're right and you're wrong.

Everybody is born with a ration of strength
which is unvarying in life,
like the length from knee to hoof of a new born colt
that bestraddles the shifting world
complete with defence mechanisms and uncertainty.

There is nothing humble or hopeful in the stance;
you have only been dropped in the grass
for some unknown reason,
it is probably spring and the trees are sleek
with their recurring foliage. There is apple blossom
in other people's gardens.
The universities are spilling over
with beautiful girls and boys with unbelievable hair
and rich mummies and daddies
that somehow never seem to intrude, but supply them
with blank cheques and accounts in Switzers and
    Brown Thomas.
It used to be possible to have your food delivered
you could ring up the shop
for a pound of spaghetti or a yard of tulle.
Now it turns out
to be a Black Maria
and the police are dunderheads and quite ready
to accept you as a criminal
when you are prepared to say with oriental courtesy
that you are really sorry, will pay back the money even

if it means that your children will go hungry.
You accept the fact that the north is the north
the south the south, that the seagulls come inland
to eat garbage at dawn.

When the streets are empty
save for drunks and office cleaners
– the night watchmen sleep in their little tents –
they have watched right through the night
with nothing in their heads;
for how else, watchmen, could the night be endured –
would you watch the little opening always
for someone who will not come
and share thin shelter against the prevailing winds?
The prevailing wind in the town is your own
    breathing
that comes blue and sporadic, and if fossilised
would be glorious like parchment.

You have read from the scribe Ani the Book of the
    Dead
in dyes that were made from mosses and flowers,
your ear has adjusted to the even distribution
of flutes and strings,
and wind out of isolated knowledge makes a musical
    whole;

the cemetery is neat graves under graves
there is always more room for a corpse,
once consecrated you're home and dried.
If you are rich
you can have a pyramid erected on top of you

or a whole fleet of angels,
designed by someone like Oisin Kelly,
or a sculptor friend of one of the Guinnesses;
the skeleton is not all that vulnerable
and still keeps its human and recognisable contours,
there is absolutely no reason
to confuse it with the bones of a hare
or something other than a creature
with an immortal soul.

Eighties

He Tries To Understand But Cannot

He tries to understand but cannot
how writing books means lots and lots of time
away from him. He loves her for
the little marks she makes on paper,
shouts his approval in every bar in town.
But when he sees her sitting at her desk
he wants to kill her.
He tries and tries but cannot understand.

One day he came home rotten drunk
and screaming, Where the fuck's my dinner?
He yelled so loud the neighbours came
but he was strong and they were weak,
they ran.

He tries to understand but cannot.
It is beyond him how at first he loved her
for the little marks on paper that she made
but didn't realise how come they got there,
that sometimes she must sit and write them down.

Alas this story has no ending.
Eventually he'll kill her, that she knows.
With slender hands he'll throttle her
and boast about her writings in the town.

The Scattering of The Ashes
for Anna and Bill

I.

The grass that's flattened by the orchestra of wind
lies polished for the tenderness of hand,
the stroking of this well-trod shoulder,
not green but yellow and anything but pleasant.
Named downs they lift to the lined horizon,
shrug off the factory town below;
like grey uncarded hair
smoke straggles from the pear-shaped chimneys.

II.

And there are seven, connected
by blood or breath, with bowed heads
and gammon cheeks, who falter unevenly in the
    dried-out ruts
as brother holds brother in a cardboard box;
confused in his own flesh he offers it windward
his fingers ringed by the twine –
it's barely big enough to parcel
an inexpensive clock.
Of what do they chat or whom do they discover
in the this and that of ceremony?

III.

Pulverised bone is grey and carbon to the touch;
adheres to palms and the edges of nails.
As each shakes forth his individual veil,
the wind gusts and divides the matrices;
the immediate matter is settled with the dust
that curious beasts have recently disturbed.

IV.
Married, long divorced, a couple
in this funeral of chords
unreels a filament of memory.
It's a safe bargaining with the merchandise of years;
the spit-on-the-hand, the luck-penny that's returned.

Berkshire/Dublin 1981

Spring Song

O the lacuna of spring –
flowers, sun, buds, birds nesting.
But in my mirror peers Ms Death –
Meat face, she is.
But O the lacuna of spring.

It's a long street this death.
I see my grandfather walking his Fido
'Come along, little doggie, come along.'

Grandpa died in '52
and he is walking the street of my death
with his Fido.

He says 'what a queer life you lead as a poet'.
He doesn't call me a poetess
because he has learnt in his deathness
that Sappho started the game –
Sappho of so many lovers
all as pretty as butterflies
and she was a poet.

The tom cat has left his spor.
It smells of grapefruit in the early morning kitchen.
New life! New life! New lives for old.
(When I was a lass I also waited in the market place
but no one told me how to rub the lamp.)

However I salute the fathers of my children
though nary a one could care
that in this spring of my ancient years
I type by the cat house:
Oh, the lacuna of spring.

The Flight

The flight was inevitable
(she couldn't remember much
except she wound up in a grotto).
Somewhere in the blue light
a statue was there – water
also was involved –
it made a curious noise
like small feet running
and she was sick – eclipsed
in a venom of nausea.

The vomit kept coming
excluding breath as though her lungs
were parceled up against her throat.

There was a rocking sound
of some coarse music in her head
each pain had its own gender
taking in turn its male or female form,
making sport of her own child's body.

She felt she could hear the grass growing,
the growling of stones
or feel the tilt of the earth
as it tried to shoulder her off.
Sometimes she knelt or squatted.
As dawn ventured would have made a weird triangle
(had anyone seen her).

But of course, the one person
on whose door she knocked,
half-dressed, be-slippered,
soutane-less, certainly Godless
didn't want to know, so did not see.

Sometimes the earth may give a jerk,
when all the creatures communicate;
there may be a hint of cows
the bleat of a January lamb
the birth of another unwanted baby
the death of a girl and her child.

I'm Trying to Tell You, Mr Justice Lynch

i.m. The Kerry Babies Tribunal

My feet drag, it is my seventh month
and eyes, all eyes my enemies.
I must be furtive, sly
as if to hide the pumping heart
of a stolen bird. (My bird,
that other, flies further to the horizon.
Can I ride you now
like the wren on the eagle's back,
let the sun scorch my wings?
There is no quiet breath
for my wind-blown feathers
to make my white skin glow.)

The bird pants – each
his own calender – each his own first
fretful step into an unknown
inquisition – to die or live
without a dream – without a story
for each should have his tale eventually.

So when my time is come
I will stand in the sour grass
of a long gone summer
and, with the first cry, see
my rivers snake the scutch
as red is to black in an April's dawn.

Into Madness

for K.M.

If I must go, I must go quickly
To the place where the doors have no handles.
For they have chased me there, branch-men,
Buses, teenagers with spiky hair,
Chain mail – *dit* Fascist – pardon – maybe it's me.

If I go then, it is to be seen gone, known
To have left – what? The Italian café in Fenian Street,
York Street, all the pubs that won't serve me,
Or simply the dangers of the past, one circle in my brain
Spotlights these to zero – no – maybe it's me
Sheltering in my own madness. Is insanity
Survival? Or less? An escape from living on the dole,
Simply, which, in twenty minutes will be spent on
     drink?

Please do not stop me, ask me to think
But allow me my special concentration, the spiral
     of anger
Which orchestrates my panic, my stress – a cadenza –
This I must perfect, repeat, to give me time.

St Brigid's Day 1989

The women's calls
go up across the lake.
On this still day their voices
whip the air – staccato notes
behind the reed-hushed margin.

Winter is writing out its past
before its time
while they trail the shore
anxious to garner reeds
for Brigid's Cross, bending
in all their different flesh-shapes
like shoppers to admire a bud,
an early primrose, a robin
shrilly calling to its mate.

Although I gather rushes
like these strolling women
I'm made conscious
of the decades that divide us
and that I should be celebrating
Brigid in her strength
of fruitfulness and learning.

I can only offer her the satchel of these years,
I too, will make a cross, for luck and irony.
Amongst the witches coven I will raise my glass
so my children's children's children
will gather rushes for her turning.

Don't Go Down That Road

for John McLachlan

John said, as sons will,
With some concern and disapproval,
Don't go down that road.

A Christmas of tinsel and turmoil,
it was, until
the year split like an envelope,
and opened the wounds –
a half-plucked pheasant,
the turkey carcass like a rusting car.

Oh my God, are the rocks
grinding themselves to powder
are the scars screaming their pain
to the wind to cut them clean.

An old man feeds his bullocks,
knee deep in Monaghan mud,
hocks, splashed, joints
locked in anticipation.
Life goes on, they say,
willy-nilly, as though you could toss
the earth like a coin
and it didn't matter how it fell.

But I had gone down that road
of ivy and torn dreams,
my children around me – men and women –
nervous of me and arrogant as stars,
knowing that I'd disgrace them once again.

He said, I shouldn't have gone that road,
but I didn't listen, O, I didn't listen.

Nineties

Matisse Woman

The woman emerges
two-dimensional.
She presses into the wall,
slides off her clothes,
removing the cover
of the transfer.
But the sudden hues remain –
polka dots – the splash
of blood on the vase –
peonies, violets
sprayed against the curtain.
She smiles, her body opens
to produce a child.
Where has he gone? they ask.
She points to the belly

but there is no birth
only the shadows of leaves
tracing the twilight
of her skin.

She Tried To Be A Woman Twice

She tried to be a woman
brought him the oranges of love,
on trays of malachite,
coddled the egg
exactly as he liked it.
She ghosted an evergiving
smile – a wraith above the bed,
bleached her mind
to match his evenly,
shivered at his touch.

Branded thus she bore him sons,
tidied away the genes,
when the last one came.
She withdrew gently as night
proves itself into day, knowing
for a brief time her dawn.

The second time she wearied to his will
her skull expanded, her heart
bled its secrets into his sieve.
Her days lay down upon each other,
her protective soul, no longer
weatherproof, let in the storm.

The empty chair, uneaten meats,
the angry shoulders
told their history – her story
wandered off – a body into sleep.

Moments

for Edward McLachlan

No moon slides over Harcourt Terrace.
The canal is black. The barracks
crouches on her left.
She sees the child. He holds his coat
across his chest. On his hands,
old socks blunt his fingers.
The handle of his fishing net
has snapped.

Sleep escapes the old woman
on her angry couch. Such images
assault, torment and tease
the sense of her.
Time rolls back on its silent wheels,
empties itself into moments.

How many guilts can one human endure.
One human in all the world, alone
one man or woman holding moments
of a child running, holding shut his coat
with socks on his hands.

Song of the African Boy

Oh Sligo, my Africa,
I am black
and my mother
brings home the shopping
in two Quinnsworth bags.

Oh Sligo, my Africa,
I own a donkey
and a pair of runners,
did I tell you I was black
and my mother does the shopping?

Oh Sligo, my Africa,
I knew you my father
from darkest Islington
for as long as it took
to drop your semen
into my mother's womb.

And I shall grow tall and black
in Sligo, my Africa
and the bolen will slip
from the harbour
to the blunting of the sea.

I will let my mother
walk those long miles
from Quinnsworth
while I shrug my shoulders
at the feet
of the continent's shelf.

Oh Sligo, my Africa,
break the long silence
that is my quarter.

My mother doesn't chide me
because the palms of my hands
are pink
but I know how she feels
on the long road
when the yellow iris nods.

He Begs Her To Stay

Please stay, the chevaux de frise
won't last forever.

She can't listen. She thinks
I can't lie here day after day
while the mind fingers
the barriers.

We must enter together
the boutique of loneliness
and fill our baskets.

Two Lessons in Anatomy: York Street, Dublin

Lesson 1 – i.m. The X Case.

The father of the pregnant girl
has lost his temper – their bodies
reflected in the armour of rush hour traffic.
Two people from one kitchen.

She rubs her eyes like a cat
polishing its face with a single paw.
His anger spins from the bones of his shoulders
with the crescendo of his curses.

She backs away, knocking into students,
bruising her ankle on the pedal of a bike.
She will go to that nowhere place
where decisions bang around in her head.
I wonder will she remember the time
the moth was banging against the electric bulb
and how she climbed on that wobbly chair
to cup the insect in her palm
to throw it from the open window.

Lesson II

The woman upstairs is being beaten.
Her screams jangle across the street
where windows in the College of Surgeons
black out one by one. Students
are filtering home to their digs
in Rathmines or Ranelagh
and the air is left untroubled
by the cry for help
that no lessons in anatomy can fathom.

Dancing With Beezy In Jordan's Pub

With country and western suit
gangster tie, bell bottoms
he sings to us

Dancing with Beezy in Jordan's

As gangster guest
in this company
the soft shoe rhythm
tidies away the throb:

Will you waltz, my love,
Will you waltz with me
again

We women talk of rain
and chemotherapy.

Three Ages to Midnight

She took the cross-bar
all the way to Kilcock
on the midnight hour
of Plough Monday
conceived a son
carried him back
by the light
of the Milky Way
born nine moons after
on the hill of Annamult.

At the periphery of Clare
they bundled into a dance-hall
Are ye from Mars, married, single,
lost? No she's married to midnight
on the Prairie by Ennistymon
and lives with Sean
the cowgirl's man.

She is the oldest witch in Cloughboley
grandmother to midnight
callgirl to the moon.
She eats hare's feet and atropine
manages badly on her income
of Bulls Blood and Kerosene.

Ghost Story

Beyond the horse-hair rain
on the windscreen,
the hare jumps –
a fleeting nod from the rhodedendrons.

There's only a headlight glint
between driver and corpse –
so perfect, so other-worldly,
you can't blame the rain for everything.

Next night the driver went that road,
the rain-man flagged him down
in his old torn mac, he thumbed a lift
and they drove together silently.

The driver saw the dark brown fur
on the rain-man's wrist,
watched the man's ears growing,
the nose twitching.
Please don't do this to me,
the driver said.

Aha, said the man in the long torn coat
arched his beautiful back and sniffed the air.
You can drop me by the rhodedendrons,
You can't blame the rain for everything.

Blow In

She came
with her pile of books
her manuscripts
her published works.

She took her stance
the men parenthesised their pints
to stare. Some welcomed,
others shifted. Restless
crafts in their harbour.

So brash in her folly
she thought to take
the heavy sea and storm
it into her breast. To lift
the slap, the suck.

Did she not come
to learn the ABC
the classroom sums
how two and two don't always
make the tidy count.

No one moved until
she tried to prove
she was the college girl
she'd learn and poise her pen
but listless in this knowledge
they split her like a log.

Yet for quite some time
they took her in.
Bowing to the tradition
of hospitality –
guests are welcome for a time –
when you've drunk their wine
you ought to leave
with dignity. Take with you
the coat they've offered you
and wear it right.

Playing Tennis With Eamonn

If, as is the view, tennis is sinful
I sinned on the back line
for twenty double faults.
O Lord forgive me for sinning on the back line
of the asphalt tennis court
in Tuosist, County Kerry.

Eamonn, a stocky lad of some ten years
beat me six love, six love
And I in my eighteenth year
not all that nimble on my pins
took love easy on the back line
on the back line of the tennis court
in Tuosist, County Kerry.

But in the third set, oh the third set
with my splintering back hand
I had him on the gallop.
Haring from one side of the court
to the other, Eamonn, ten year old Eamonn
was hard put with his returns.
And my lobs – you've never seen lobs like them
they soared like gulls in the pouring rain
far above the tennis court, the asphalt tennis court
in Tuosist, County Kerry.

And after my twentieth double fault
my serves skimmed into the right hand corner
creating pebbles of asphalt to scatter in the flood,
globules of asphalt, craters of asphalt
bullets of asphalt as the water logged ball

slithered and Eamonn, gibbering with ten year
   old rage
played fast and loose with forbidden curses
cursing rain, me, asphalt and Tuosist.

I picked up my crutches and tottered home
to the cornerstone of the Kingdom,
the soaking corner of the Beara Peninsula,
the wettest corner of Western Europe.

Eamonn pissed off to his dinner.

Cynic On The Rock

for Dermot Seymour

I watch him watching the sea
I've come from a city
of glass domes, streets
dancing with useless sentences
I want to tell him
out there the mind jumps and scatters
a townscape of no walls.

He bows to the crescendo of the gale
the sea shakes out its petticoats.

What can I say to him?
That I am trying to buy time
create a shell in this white horizon
to find in this enormity of sea and sky
a jot, a new word at the very end
of the dictionary.

Tell me, he says, without turning,

Is there wind in Belfast?

My Old Aberdeen

The heel of a shoe
taps three four three four.
Someone dances
in someone else's head.

A voice cries:
Come on Mary, sing
Give her a hand, everyone.

In a cathedral of silence
she sings:

My Old Aberdeen
and no one wants to know.

An old man with a curious limp says:
it would make a dog think.

Nothing Else
for Nicholas McLachlan

Cloonagh, below the sweep
of Ardtrasna, a pocket unfilled
where the hill rises. Trá Bhán
the beach where the barge buckled
in '95 and bothered us
with possibilities. Trá Bhán
no longer white but sheeted over
with shloch and erannach and rock
limestone steps to the blow-hole
under the alt, is the end of the road
and nothing else.

Above this crescent
I share my house with time
and nothing else
gaze at the pictures of my children
who have treated me well
for my imagination
but pass me by as the wind passes the house
and takes its sigh with it.

Dog Ear

I am turning my death over
like a page in a book
I dog-ear it.
I need to remember the place.

Post Card

I drift to sleep,
thinking of the blow-hole under the alt
and wondering about a sea lion
I once met.

I dream then of the window
and fingers walking.
A post card is pushed
under the door.
It comes in with the rain
which obliterates the message.

January 1st '95, The Party's Over

The party ended yesterday.
Pocket whiskey gone the roads,
fundamentals packed.

The sea in party frock
punched the air, slapped in '95.
The mountain moved across the light.

The cat crossed the moon at 2 a.m.
shirking the secret of dawn.
The mind won't clear that easy.

The party ended yesterday
pocket whiskey gone the roads,
the new light leaves you unprepared.

The Dead Child's Arm Washed Up
On The Beach

The dog brought
the arm of the child
ulna to radius

fingers wrested
from the ocean's pillow.

The dog took the bones
to the other child.

He who lives
thinking of that other he
the child

who picked up the bones
with the dead hand
reaching ulna

crossing the radius
to the wrist
of that other child.

White the bones
of the children, white
the lace of the sea's kiss.

Hale-Bopp

i.m. Martin Healy , d. 5th March 1997

I'll sit one more day
in the chair, or even
walk out to test the night
to hover in the wet grass,
trying to catch sight
of a comet.

Cuckoo On Top Of The Protestant Church, Dugort

Cuckoo, Cuckoo, Cuculus Canorus,
remarkable bird. I heard you
yesterday winging your way
to drop your bastard egg
in someone else's house.

Who's afraid of your cuckoo-spit
your lady's smock your
ragged robin dress?

Cuckoo, Cuckoo, Cuculus Canorus,
from bed to bed hop skip
and jump. Frog-hopper
Protestant church-goer
over the trees and up.

Cuckoo, Cuckoo, yes
I heard you yesterday
here there and everywhere
summer-harbinger, bad bird,
liar, egg-dropper.

I like your nerve,
Cuculus Canorus,
gate crasher
percher on steeples.
Such selfishness,
such panache
never in the one place
twice.

No Return

They tried to recapture
the days of Leonard Cohen.
Dylan, the Beatles
as they downed a bottle of Bush,
sang unmusically, fell
into the bed.

It was a belated effort –
two desperadoes on a sinking ship
no pirate of passion
to storm the bulwark.
They laughed at last,
remembering the mornings
of Black Russian cigarettes.

Mad Mrs Sweeney

For one whole year
I've watched Mad Sweeney
above in his branch.

He has forgotten how to fly
and stares down at me.
Occasionally he spits.

Today I plucked up courage
to address him.

Mad Sweeney, I said,
I am madly in love with you.

If you'd just bend down that wing
and give me a hike

I'd be up and away,
space shuttle to the moon.

He fluffs his plumage
in that acid way he has

strops his beak
on an outgoing twig.

Well at least shake down a feather
and I'll culture it
with a ball of seaweed

and when it has grown full size
I'll fly to the top of your tree

and be mad Mrs Sweeney
gone in the head but heart whole.

Grainnuaile's Tower Kildavnet, Achill

Eyrie on the storm's rim
breakneck descent
mist mystery, heel
of the sound – one
of her many hides.
Wild woman – high perch.
They built them strong then
castles, women, walls.

Seasons

Autumn

Weeds through the curragh's ribs
Grass on the jinnet's hames
Rust on the tall ship's anchor

God's acre splits
Cow moans, tumbles
Kestrel defines the wind

Arranged in this landscape
I await the wound of winter
The coming of the geese

Spring

The moon aligns the sun
The ocean gathers

The weeds search for light
The ring of the eye expands

The scar of the torrent knits
The boulders flatten

The hares rut
The rhisomes shiver

The loam breathes
The earthworms sing

Ewe at the Corner

Every day she is at the corner
with her February twins;
a mother at the cross roads
waiting for the school bus.

Poor sheep confused
mud-black face
fleece in tangles.

Down at the harbour
they are turning over the boats
whipping the winter
out of the holds.
There's a wink of sea-strife
on the dunes.
The Northern hemisphere
races from spring to spring.

Back in the cities
mothers entangled with children
are waiting for the school bus.